SEQUOIA
NATIONAL PARK
An Illustrated History

by Sandra L. Keith

SEQUOIA KINGS CANYON NATIONAL PARKS

■

Produced for Guest Services, Inc. by

SEQUOIA
COMMUNICATIONS

Sequoia Communications
Santa Barbara, California

■

Editor: Nicky Leach
Design: Adine Maron
Production Assistance: Marcus Graczyk
Type: Graphic Traffic
Map: Karen Hubbard

Printed in Hong Kong
First printing 1989

ISBN: 0-917859-96-0

■

*Front Cover: Looking out
towards the Great Western
Divide from Moro Rock,
Sequoia National Park.
Title Spread: Mount Whitney,
the highest peak in
the contiguous United States,
as seen from Sequoia
National Park.*

■

Acknowledgements

We would like to thank Glen Becker and Ramona Goodge of Guest Services for their help and enthusiasm for this book project, and Ron Green of Guest Services who provided some of the photography. Several people at Sequoia and Kings Canyon National Park Service headquarters were invaluable: Bill Tweed, for his review of the manuscript and helpful input; Larry Waldron, for his early suggestions about the text; and Ellen Seely in the historic photograph collection, for her great patience in locating historic photographs for us. A last thank you is due to Maryann at the Tulare Public Library for sharing the information about the park found in the library's collection of George Stewart's personal papers.

■

Photography

FRANK BALTHIS: 5; CARR CLIFTON: Inside Front, 6, 39 (top); ED COOPER: 8,11 (top), 13 (bottom), 15 (right, top, bottom), 42; JEFF GNASS: 25 (bottom); GUEST SERVICES, INC: 13 (top), 38 (right), 46, 47, Back Flap; PHILIP HYDE: 10, 41, Back Cover; RANDY MORGENSON: 36 (top), 40 (top); NATIONAL PARK SERVICE, SEQUOIA NATIONAL PARK: 18, 20, 22, 23, 24, 26, 28, 29, 30, 31, 32, 33, 44 (top photos); OAKLAND MUSEUM: 19; PAT O'HARA: 2, 12, 14, 30, 34, 35 (top), 48; GLENN VAN NIMWEGEN: 15 (top left), 36, 45; TULARE PUBLIC LIBRARY, VISALIA: 30 (right); KATHLEEN NORRIS COOK: Cover; KENNAN WARD: 9, 11 (bottom), 35 (bottom), 36 (bottom), 37 (bottom), 38 (left), 39 (bottom), 40 (bottom left), 43, 44 (bottom).

CONTENTS

■
An old cabin with Farewell Canyon in the distance, Mineral King, Sequoia National Park.

Chapter One

In Praise of the Big Trees

■
Opposite: The mighty sequoia trees of Sequoia National Park and (above) a cluster of snow plants.

There is no way to prepare the senses for the awe-inspiring reality of California's giant sequoias. Likening them to other trees is inaccurate, photos cannot capture their dimension, and descriptions fall short. So overwhelming is their presence that first-time onlookers stand slack-jawed and unbelieving. Normal trees simply do not bear such girth. Nor stand so tall. Nor possess such magnetism. But then these are not normal trees. These trees are vegetal kings—the largest living things on Earth.

Giant sequoias—also known as "big trees"—are one of three species of redwoods in existence today. As a race, they have survived the dinosaurs, the great mountain uplifting, and the Ice Age. Many sequoias standing today are snag-topped, fire-scarred, out of plumb, or burned through. And still they live. Their deeply furrowed trunks rise from elephantine bases with circumferences in excess of 100 feet; their limbs are often half-ton appendages which, in any eastern forest, would be heralded as champions in their own right. Their crowns can stand more than 300 feet high. Some are nearly 3,000 years old. They are, quite simply, extraordinary. But achieving such size and longevity required some remarkable adaptations.

Because fungi and insect invasions are known tree-killers, the sequoia needed a way to keep them at bay. Tannin was the answer. The sequoia's bark and wood are impregnated with this astringent substance, which is both an effective decay inhibitor and insect repellent. Tannin also gives the tree its distinctive color—bright cinnamon-red. The chemical is such a good preservative that even when one of the giants falls to earth, it takes decades, and sometimes centuries, for it to rot away. This is not surprising since even tiny taste buds are fussy, and no creeping thing in its right mind ever took a second bite of anything as bitter as a tannin-laced sequoia.

Fire is another problem. It is, of course, a certainty that blazes will sweep through the groves from time to time. So the tree is insulated against the inevitable by an asbestos-like bark that is at least a foot thick and nearly devoid of pitch—the flammable agent that

■

*Dogwood in bloom in Giant
Forest.*

ignites so readily in other conifers. Even
so, infernos sometimes leave a giant sequoia
with a blackened bole or hollowed-out trunk.
Not to worry: this successfully adapted tree
can heal itself. If even a fraction of the cir-
cumference remains intact, the cambium, or
cell-producing layer, will grow new wood
over the wound, eventually effecting a cure
so complete that only if the tree falls or is
cut down will evidence of past fires come
to light.

As a result of all this, the giant sequoia is
virtually indestructible. It would most likely
live forever were it not for one area of vulner-
ability: the tree has no taproot. Instead, it
is anchored to earth by a vast network of
surface roots which, even at the tree's base,
grow only four or five feet into the ground.
And even though the roots spread laterally
in all directions—sometimes as much as 200
feet or more—the knobby maze is easily
undermined by spring floods or altered
drainage patterns that occasionally leave
the giant perched atop a gaping hole. When
that happens, the sequoia tries to balance
its bulk by sending out huge limbs on the
side opposite the erosion problem. Other
times, it builds a buttress by slowing or
stopping all growth on the unstabilized side
while adding new wood—in prodigious
amounts—along the base of the stable side.
Sometimes this works and the sequoia con-
tinues to flourish and produce fertile seed.
Other times it does not, and with a groan
that reverberates throughout the grove, the
great red tree releases its fragile hold on the
earth and crashes to the forest floor.

Nevertheless, the exceedingly well-adapted
sequoia tree appears to have developed this
shallow root system in response to both its
tall, narrow shape and the thin mountain
soils of the Sierra Nevada. The sequoia is in-
extricably linked to its chosen environment.

THE HOME OF THE SEQUOIA

Standing or fallen, one fact remains: the
giant sequoia is the unrivaled monarch of
the forest. In their entirety, the Big Trees
cover almost 37,000 acres of the Sierra
Nevada's central section, growing along the
western slope in a rather discontinuous
belt nearly 260 miles long—though never
more than 15 miles wide—and seldom
straying above or below their favored eleva-
tions of 4,500 to 7,500 feet above sea level.

In all, there are 75 groves. Some claim but a few trees; others boast as many as 20,000.

The giants of the realm live in Sequoia and Kings Canyon National Parks. It is here that the ruddy goliaths reach their grandest stature, boasting dimensions that defy the imagination. King of them all is the General Sherman tree, the largest living thing on Earth. The 2,500-year-old soars nearly 275 feet skyward, boasts a base-diameter of almost 37 feet, and excluding its ponderous branches (one of which is 6.8 feet in diameter), weighs a hefty 1,385 tons.

Yet the General is not content to simply rest on its laurels. It was a behemoth last year; it will be even larger next year. And almost as though there were some sort of contest taking place or prize money to be won, the tree works at retaining its title, each year adding another millimeter to its girth. When totaled, this seemingly minute amount equals 40 cubic feet of new wood, a feat that gives the General Sherman yet another claim to fame: fastest-growing measured tree in the world.

Perhaps the one characteristic that makes the giant sequoia such a memorable species is not that any single tree is largest, oldest, or tallest, but that each one stands with such regal dignity. Individually, they bespeak strength. And patience. And tenacity. Collectively, they reduce the visitor to silence. Here are trees equal to their history. They have stood against adversity and won. Many standing today claim B.C. birth dates, and their ancestry spans the ages. For these are a relict species—survivors of a titan race which, at its zenith, covered much of the Northern Hemisphere.

PREHISTORIC BEHEMOTHS

Exactly when the first sequoias raised their crowns towards the sun is uncertain, though fossil records indicate their closest ancestral relatives existed at least 175 million years ago. These ancient redwoods were prolific, and in time, their many species became the predominant members of the mixed deciduous-conifer forests that blanketed Europe, Asia, the Arctic, and North America.

But then everything changed. The mountains pushed upward; volcanoes spewed out tons of ash and lava; and the sun scorched low-lying basins where the red-

■
Left: The General Sherman Tree is the largest tree in the world. Below: Sequoia trees need fire in order to propagate. Fire scarring is a common sight.

woods had once thrived. With winters now too cold and summers too hot and dry, the giant trees began disappearing from their ancestral range, and by 50 million years ago most had either vanished or become increasingly restricted.

And then the ice came—a great, creeping chill that sliced through soil, bulldozed bedrock, and carved canyons out of granite. Even the giant trees were no match for the overriding tonnage that bore down on them, and when at last the ice melted northward, it revealed a land nearly scraped of life. But not entirely. Two genera of the redwoods survived in what is now California.

The taller and slimmer *Sequoia sempervirens,* or coast redwood, grew only along the Pacific Coast; the fatter, somewhat shorter *Sequoiadendron giganteum,* or giant sequoia, lived nowhere else but along the Sierra Nevada's western slope. And though each consisted of but a single species in a severely restricted range, they were still there, spreading their massive canopies toward the clouds and hushing the voice of the wind.

■
Opposite: The House Group of sequoias. Above: Fallen sequoias reveal their massive root system and are good fun for young climbers. Left: Stately sequoias guard the Generals Highway near Giant Forest.

Sierra Nevada Geology

The oldest rocks in the Sierra Nevada originated in a marine environment. Easy to see why. During the Paleozoic era, 225 million years ago, this part of California was covered by an inland sea whose shallow waters lay atop innumerable bands of sedimentary and volcanic rock. But then the Earth's crustal plates began overriding one another, and as they did, the rock layers became fractured, faulted, and folded into an underground mountain range. In time, intense pressure within the Earth heated the bedrock, transforming it into a mass of oozing liquid. Just above the liquid zone, relative heat and pressure did some transforming of their own, turning limestone into marble and other sediments into gneiss and schist, and by the time the whole mass had cooled, the Sierra Nevada batholith was in place—a great granitic slab ready to be born.

It lay there for unknown millennia, topped over time by tons of sediment and rock. Then 80 to 85 million years ago, pressures within the Earth changed once again, and as they did so the granitic block was bent, twisted, and squeezed anew until at last, released from its dark womb, the ancient Sierra rose to greet a sun-washed sky. But the virgin range soon altered shape. During the following millenia, rivers and streams downcut the low-slung mountains, washing most of the sediment cap into a small sea in the Central Valley, and by the time all was said and done, the ancient Sierra was little more than low foothills.

SEISMIC ACTION

No matter. Step three was on its way. Volcanoes and seismic forces were about to change the face of the land forever. Rhyolite flows poured over what remained of the ancient Sierra crest, ash filled river streams, lava overtopped lava until it reached depths of as much as a half-mile in the northern Sierra. And then the earthquakes came. Jolt upon jolt. Rumble atop rumble. As the Earth heaved, the bedrock block snapped along its eastern edge, and as it did the great granite slab tilted, upended,

and began rising upward. With each cataclysmic gyration, the fault block rose higher, and each time the rivers kept pace, entrenching themselves ever deeper into the face of the Sierra until in the end, they had carved their way through solid rock to form deep V-shaped canyons.

As the Sierra lifted almost perpendicularly on the east, the climate began to cool. No more did winter snows melt during summer months, and eventually great ice fields formed in the range's highest reaches. When the icy fingers headed downward they took the paths of least resistance—the river canyons—and by the time they melted back upslope, the canyons had been remodeled into broad, flatbottomed valleys whose distinct U-shape would forever bespeak their history.

It was finished at last—a range so magnificently dissected and disarrayed that the Indians who later inhabited its vast reaches claimed it was a land of "rock on rock and snow on snow." Early Spanish explorers christened it *una gran sierra nevada*—a great snowy mountain range. John Muir eulogized it as "the Range of Light." To geologists it is simply a fault block mountain, 450 miles long and 60 to 80 miles wide, whose many resplendent peaks, barren domes, and glacial stairways are all attached to the same granitic bedrock. Whatever its title, the Sierra Nevada is an imposing rock wall which, in its entirety, looks like a gigantic ocean wave surging toward Nevada. And along its southeastern edge, just where the wave reaches its apex, is the incomparable 14,495 foot-high Mount Whitney—the highest peak in the contiguous states.

■ *Opposite: Whitney Portal at Mount Whitney—at 14,495', the highest mountain in the contiguous United States. Top Left: Exfoliating Sierra granite. Top Right: Mount Muir (14,015') in John Muir wilderness, boundary of Sequoia National Park. Above: Hamilton Creek, Angel Wings seen from a high Sierra trail.*

Chapter Two

The Creation of Sequoia National Park

■ *Opposite: Delicate dogwood blooms contrast with the rough, corklike texture of two giant sequoias. Above: Stockman Hale Tharp was shown the sequoias of Giant Forest by his neighbors in the Three Rivers area, the Potwisha Indians; he was the first white man to view the trees. The summer home that he built in the forest from a fallen giant sequoia can still be seen in Crescent Meadow.*

Although Spanish explorers are credited with discovering the coast redwoods in 1769, it was a hunter named Augustus T. Dowd who, in 1852, went down in history as the first white man to discover the Sierra Big Trees in what is now known as Calaveras Big Trees State Park. Employed to keep meat on the table for the men of Murphys, a goldrush boomtown, Dowd was far from camp and tracking a wounded grizzly when he came smack up against what must have seemed a mountain of wood. Here was the biggest tree he had ever seen, and at that particular moment nothing—not even fresh meat for supper—seemed as important as getting back to tell of his fantastic find.

Unfortunately for Dowd, tall tales were so common in the Mother Lode that his story was looked upon as nothing more than a real knee-slapper, and the harder he tried to convince, the more the men joked and ridiculed. But Dowd was undaunted. He simply bided his time till Sunday rolled around, and about the time the men were lazing around camp he stumbled into their midst, quite out of breath, and announced that he had just shot the biggest grizzly he had ever laid eyes on. It was, in fact, so huge that he needed help getting it back to camp.

The men were on their feet in an instant. After all, a jumbo grizzly would be a sight to see, and by the time Dowd headed out of camp, most of the Murphys miners were close behind. Through the chaparral they went, down across creekbeds and over ridgetops until at last, with a triumphant wave of his hand, Dowd pointed toward a mammoth tree and said, "Now, boys, do you believe my big tree story?" They did. And before long, so would the rest of the world. The *Sonora Herald* was the first to publicize Dowd's discovery. Shortly thereafter the San Francisco *Echo du Pacific* picked up the story, and within a year the great botanical find had been announced in London's *Athenaeum* and *Gardener's Chronicle*. The word was out. Scientists came to look, ponder, and measure. Promoters came with plans aplenty for making easy money. These were, after all, forest monoliths. And the most sensible thing to do was chop them down and ship them off to places where the multitudes

■

Right: The 235' General Noble Tree being felled for a World's Fair. Opposite: Scottish-born William Keith was one of a number of 19th-century artists drawn to the splendors of the Sierra Nevada. He painted this scene in Kings Canyon in 1878.

would pay to gawk. And so they did. Little more than a year after Dowd's discovery the first giant sequoia fell at the hand of man. But once on the ground, the 302-foot-long patriarch proved unmovable and the most that could be readily accomplished was to strip off whole sections of bark so they could be reassembled for a premier showing in San Francisco and, later, in New York. With the exhibit a success, ever-increasing numbers of profiteers joined the ranks of the unscrupulous. More trees were cut, a standing sequoia was divested of much of its bark, and a stupendous stump was turned into a dance floor. By 1876, entire trunk-sections were showing up at world's fairs and expositions as well as private exhibits, and though many came to view, few believed their eyes and for the most part considered the whole thing nothing more than a California hoax.

NAMING THE BIG TREE

While promoters pioneered ways to cash in on the world's largest tree, botanists battled over what to name it. Thirty years earlier the scientific community had been at odds over what to call the coast redwood, with Austrian botanist Stephen Endlicher finally proposing the tree's genus as *Sequoia* and the species *sempervirens*. But that had

been child's play compared to the war waged over naming the Sierra Big Tree. Botanists from the California Academy of Natural Sciences claimed it was of the same species as the cypress and labeled it *Taxodium giganteum*. English botanist John Lindley said it was a new genus and named it *Wellingtonia gigantea* after the Duke of Wellington. Americans, determined that no tree of theirs should be named for an Englishman, countered with *Taxodium washingtonianum* and *washingtonia californica*. Joseph Decaisne, a French botanist, said the Sierra

tree was of the same genus as the coast red-wood and should rightly be called *Sequoia gigantea.* And so it was—at least until 1938 when John Bucholz, an American botanist, pointed out the many differences between the coastal and mountain species and claimed the Sierra tree should be called *Sequoiadendron giganteum.* So far the name has stuck.

By any title, the bulky behemoths would have met their sure and certain fate. The promoters were but the first assault team, and although they destroyed many of the finest sequoias in their quest for displays and dance floors, their defilement was nothing compared to the ravages wrought by greedy lumbermen who eyeballed the tree's incredible dimensions and saw nothing more than board feet and big bucks. Hardest hit were the groves in the southern Sierra, especially those in the Kings River and Tule River watersheds. Easy to see why. The stands here were dense and close together, the trees were world-class specimens, the area was relatively accessible, and the land was easy to come by.

When California became a state in 1850, nearly all of the Sierra Nevada remained under federal control and as such was open for homesteading. All a settler had to do to acquire 160 acres of unoccupied land was to file a claim under the Homestead Act, live on the land for five years, make a few improvements, and it was his forever. There was only one drawback: the Homestead Act had been created mainly to help farmers and homesteaders and offered no provision for lumbering or grazing. Nevertheless, cunning individuals found other ways to accumulate substantial sequoia acreage. All it took was a little subterfuge and a few greedy government surveyors.

THE GREAT LAND RUSH

Under the Stone and Timber Act, a settler could obtain 160 acres, on which he was never required to live or make any improvements, for the measly sum of $2.50 an acre. This proved to be irresistible. Any lumberman desiring to hold title to far more than the allotted acreage had only to go out into the highways and byways, find the down-and-outers, or drunkards, or anyone else with either a bit of larceny in their soul or a desperate need for money, and prevail upon them to file claims on adjoining tracts —using, of course, the lumberman's funds. Consequently, many of the claims were not filed under the real names, yet whether real or false, the end result was always the same: the acreage was signed over to the lumberman, the claimants got their prearranged fee, and no one was the wiser.

The plan was varied slightly to accommodate the Swamp and Overflow Act. By law, any area listed in the survey books as at least 50 percent marsh reverted from federal to state control and could then be sold to private individuals. Again, it was ridiculously easy to circumvent the rules. All the lumberman had to do was to find a greedy surveyor, preferably in the spring when the sequoia groves were boggy with upland snowmelt, grease his palms, and the land in question was officially listed as swampland. Sometimes the lumberman bought the land himself; other times he had another do the deed for him. Either way, he added yet another section of giant trees to his burgeoning empire.

By the time the overworked and under-staffed government land office got wise to what was going on, thousands of acres of giant sequoias had passed into private hands. Most were lost forever, particularly those fraudulently purchased during the summers of 1886 and 1887 by the Kings River Lumber Company. But one section in particular was retrievable. It was called Giant Forest, and if the 40 or so members of the Cooperative Land and Colonization Association had not made one fatal mistake when filing claims on connecting tracks, the very heart of Sequoia National Park might be nothing more than a land of tombstone trunks.

THE KAWEAH COLONY

As individuals, the association members were mostly radical San Franciscans with two common goals: to be free of a capitalist society and to recruit as many as possible to their Socialist ideals. Collectively, they hoped to establish a utopian commune where they would be financially successful and completely self-sufficient. With the demand for lumber rising steadily, a logging venture in the Big Trees seemed the answer. In the autumn of 1885, individual members of the association entered the Visalia Land Office and filed claims on adjoining tracts in Giant Forest, collectively obtaining 6,000 acres of prime timberland. There was, however, one fly in the ointment: most of the claimants had listed the same San Franciscan address. The local land officer, suspicious that the colonists were but a front for a lumber baron, called for investigation.

Unable to quickly unravel what was going on, the investigator did the next best thing and encouraged the general land office commisioner to temporarily suspend from sale a great swatch of Sierra timberland, including the area that contained Giant Forest. Although the colonists considered the investigation a setback, they were positive that their claims would eventually be verified and spent the winter enlisting new members. By the spring of 1886, still certain that the land would soon be theirs, they reorganized as the Kaweah Commonwealth Company and set up a tent camp on the North Fork of the Kaweah River. By summer, their on-site ranks had swelled to 160 people; by autumn, they were cutting a wagon road toward Giant Forest.

■
Kaweah colonists working on Colony Mill Road, late 1880s.

THE UNITED STATES OF AMERICA,
To all to whom these presents shall come, Greeting:

■

Top: Following California statehood in 1850, homesteaders and loggers flooded the southern Sierra. This 1870s homesteading certificate is typical of the many that were issued to settlers in the mid-19th century. Above: Logging continued long after Sequoia National Park was created. Here, a sequoia stump is dramatically blasted apart at Converse Basin in 1905.

Perhaps their greatest undoing was that they were not alone in making unwarranted inroads into the southern Sierra. Anyone and everyone who could find their way along the precipitous cliffs or through granite gorges was using the range as he saw fit. Cattlemen grazed their stock in the sequoia forests; sheepherders turned thousands of sheep, or "wooly lawnmowers" as John Muir called them, loose in the high meadows. And all the while, the giant trees were being cut, legally and illegally, and their brittle lumber turned into fence posts and grape stakes. It was time for Little Boy Blue to come blow his horn. And so he did. His name was George W. Stewart—and his horn was the editorial page of the *Visalia Delta.*

GEORGE STEWART: CHAMPION OF THE SEQUOIAS

Like John Muir, long-time crusader for preserving the Sierra Nevada, and Yosemite in particular, George Stewart had for many years been waging a campaign in favor of protecting the Big Trees of Fresno and Tulare counties. Even as a young man in Visalia, Stewart had shown a strong affinity for trees, and joined the Woodsmen of the World, an international group dedicated to forest preservation. His editorials condemning destructive logging practices started to appear in 1878, when he took over as editor of the *Visalia Delta.* By 1880, he was actively pushing for passage of a bill that would set aside the upper Kern and Kaweah watersheds as well as most of the Kings River country as inviolate for all time. The bill, much of it drafted by John Muir and presented in Congress by California Senator John F. Miller, was never taken seriously, mostly because the area set aside was so extensive and great swatches of it were already in private hands.

It was time to do or die. By late 1887, the Kaweah colonists' wagon road was still inching toward Giant Forest, and to make matters worse, they had gained the support of the *Tulare Times,* which pointed out that valley towns would benefit greatly from both the lumber coming off the mountain and the tourists passing through on their way to the mountain. On top of that, the new secretary of the interior, John Noble, had called for yet another investigation of the Kaweah members' claims, and Stewart, unsure of what the outcome would be, initiated his strongest campaign yet to preserve the groves still left in federal ownership.

He was not alone for long. By spring of 1889, it was obvious to everyone in the valley that lumbermen were not the only culprits to have a disastrous effect on the Sierra watershed. Sheep by the tens of thousands were now overgrazing the high country and not only were their razor-sharp hooves turning spongy meadows into impermeable deserts, but their keepers were setting untold fires in the hope of stimulating new growth for the coming year. So many drastic changes in the Sierra uplands resulted in drastic changes in the ecosystem in the valley below, and farmers once assured of a steady supply of water were now faced with springtime flooding and summer drought. To members of the local County Grange, there seemed but one solution: rally behind Stewart. And so they did.

In the autumn of 1889, leading residents of Tulare, Fresno, and Kern counties met in Visalia and agreed unanimously to petition Congress to establish a national park in the vicinity of Mount Whitney. Adding fuel to their flame was the fact that private individuals as well as the State of California had recently tried to purchase acreage in Grant Grove—site of the world's third largest tree—an area which had been withdrawn from sale in 1880 and which, if something was not done soon, would revert to the open market and be sold. With time ticking away, members stumped the valley, gathering signatures by the hundreds. The petition went off to Washington—and then, though no one ever knew exactly what took place, was not seen again until two years later.

THE FIGHT FOR PRESERVATION

In May of 1890 the unthinkable happened. The general land office commissioner placed back on the market a section of the land suspended following the Kaweah colonists' original claims. The rush was on, and within two weeks most of the acreage was in private hands. Then rumors began circulating that yet another section of those withdrawn lands would be put up for sale and, worse yet, it was the area that contained the Garfield Grove of giant sequoias. Incensed, Stewart shot off a telegram to Secretary

■ *Above: George Stewart, "Father of Sequoia National Park," probably in the twenties. Left: Judge Walter Fry, a Visalia resident and friend of Stewart, became the park's first unofficial superintendent prior to the establishment of the National Park Service in 1916.*

BIG TREES SAVED.

Gen. Vandever's Big Tree Park Bill
Passes the Senate.

The following Associated Press dis-
patch explains itself:

WASHINGTON, Sept. 8.—Vandever's
bill creating the sequoia national park
was reported favorably this morning by
Mr. Plumb, chairman of the senate committee on public lands. It was im-
mediately acted upon and passed with
out amendments.

In these days of tardy legislation it
seems wonderful that this bill should be
introduced in congress and passed without opposition, and then taken to the
senate—that great body of careful and
conscientious legislators—where it is
favorably reported by the committee on
public lands, then presented to the as-
sembly and passed without amendment
and without debate. The bill will be
presented to President Harrison to sign,
and there is not the least doubt but that
our chief magistrate will affix the seal of
approval to the measure. Those who
have taken an interest in the successful
passage of the bill can well congratulate
themselves with their splendid work.
The measure is only the opening wedge
for forestry legislation of the above
nature, and it is only a matter of a very
short time when every forest of giant
sequoia will be forever reserved from
private control and ruthless destruction.

The text of the bill has already been
published in the columns of the DELTA,
and it is only necessary to say that the
work of improving the park will be
shortly inaugurated, and that soon a
priceless heritage of scenic wonders,
mammoth trees, will be handed down to
posterity—a heritage that will be ap-
preciated.

■
*Above Left: A front-page head-
line in the September 11, 1890
issue of the* Visalia Delta *proclaims the news that Congress
has given its blessing to
Sequoia National Park. Above
Right: Early travelers in
Sequoia National Park
(date unknown).*

Noble at the Interior Department, arguing
that until the Kaweah colonists' claims to
Giant Forest were settled, the Garfield Grove
was the last uncontested stand of Big Trees
still in government hands.

It was time for a new petition. All during
that summer, Stewart and his determined
team enlisted the support of interested
groups and influential people, gathering
ever-increasing numbers of signatures and
securing the backing of both *Garden and
Forest* and *Forest and Streams,* whose
editors championed the cause on the East
Coast. The new petition was sent to the
Interior Department in late July and ac-
knowledged by the Department in August.
Simultaneously, that same July, Congressman William Vandever introduced a bill to
establish a public park in the area of Garfield
Grove, and along with the hundreds of local
signatures were telegrams and resolutions
signed by the American Association for the
Advancement of Science, the American
Forestry Association, Professor Gustavus
Eisen of the California Academy of Sciences, and William Waterman, governor
of California.

The moment had arrived. In late August,
word came that the bill had passed the
House of Representatives and was headed
for the Senate. Greatly encouraged, Stewart
and his team contacted their Washington
supporters, entreating them to push the bill
through in time to commemorate California's 40th anniversary as a state. On September 9th the news arrived: the Senate
had passed the bill with neither debate nor
amendment. On September 25th, President
Benjamin Harrison signed the bill creating
Sequoia National Park and much to everyone's surprise, signed another on September 30th, which not only created Yosemite
National Park to the north, but Grant Grove
National Park as well, and surprise of all
surprises, more than doubled the size of
Sequoia by reaching out to encompass Giant
Forest. It was time now for the secretary of
war to duplicate his actions at Yellowstone
in Wyoming, the country's first national
park, and send in the cavalry to keep order.

High Country Explorers

Prior to the 1860s, the southern Sierra high country was known only to the Indians, a few trappers, and a miner or two. Then, in 1864, Harvard geology professor Josiah Dwight Whitney, as director of the newly-formed California State Geologic Survey, sent a team of five men to officially survey the highest and most remote reaches of the Kings-Kaweah country. At the helm was William H. Brewer, and by the time the team's many months of work was over, they had not only explored and mapped the headwaters of the Kern, Kings, and San Joaquin Rivers, they had also discovered three of the highest peaks along the Sierra's rocky spine. One Brewer named for himself; another he called Mount Tyndall. The highest, he christened Mount Whitney.

Though the Brewer party was the first to actually investigate the southern Sierra crest, it was an explorer named Theodore S. Solomons who, in the 1890s, finally made his way into the formidable heart of the Kings Canyon backcountry. He discovered and named the Evolution Peaks, then went on to publish his findings. As word of the southern Sierra spread, the adventurous made their way into its wilds, and before long all of the major canyons had been explored, the highest peaks had been climbed, and most of the glacier-bitten landforms were wellknown. But it was only the beginning. For this was a mountain range with a mystique so magnetic, the hordes just kept coming. They come still. Some to explore; others to climb; many to simply stand in awe. But all to pay homage.

■
Above: Stone shelter on Muir Trail in the Sierra high country. Left: Backpacking on the high Sierra trail.

■

Chapter Three

The Park Comes of Age

■

Opposite: NPS Director Stephen Mather led a 1915 expedition into Sequoia National Park, accompanied by Congressman Frederick Gillett and Gilbert Grosvenor, president of the National Geographic Society. Both proved to be helpful in expanding the park. Above: Captain J.H. Dorst, who commanded the first U.S. cavalry troop to patrol Sequoia National Park in 1891.

The troops arrived at Mineral King in June of 1891. Commanded by Captain J.H. Dorst, the brass-buttoned cavalrymen were but the first of many who would spend half of each year patrolling Sequoia and General Grant parks, and even though the War Department never considered "park guarding" a military duty, it agreed to the Interior Department's request for assistance in protecting against timber thieves, sheepherders, stockmen, hunters, and squatters. Most of the Kaweah colonists were gone—moved away once Secretary Noble had ruled against their claims, and the few that had stayed behind were operating a small sawmill on 160 acres of leased land. Their wagon road toward Giant Forest was an engineering marvel, a dusty one-lane that was only nine miles short of its intended destination. Even though the Kaweah leaders had sought government compensation for their years of toil, their request had been denied. In the end, even the diehards packed up and moved away. It was the final page in a saga that had spanned six long years.

But all was still not quiet on the Sequoia front. The National Park Acts that had created Sequoia and General Grant had left huge sections of the southern Sierra watershed outside park boundaries—areas where lumbering was ever on the increase, cattle punched up field and forest, and sheep estimated to number half a million destroyed mountain meadows. In March, Congress had approved a bill allowing permanent forest reserves to be set aside solely by presidential proclamation. By late spring, both John Muir and George Stewart were agitating for a preserve that included not only the Sierra crest, but all of the headwaters therein—and that it be established before the land in question fell into private hands.

Nothing happened until October. Though no one could ever explain where it came from, the missing petition of 1889 requesting a large forest reserve in the southern Sierra suddenly appeared at the Interior Department. In November, Secretary Noble dispatched Special Land Agent B.F. Allen to investigate, and Allen responded by withdrawing from sale all the lands within the proposed area. By early 1892, the boundaries had been drawn to exclude

■

Top: U.S. employees in 1906
by the Fallen Monarch.
Above: Stephen Mather (third
from left), first director of
the National Park Service, in
Sequoia National Park with a
number of influential VIPs in
1927. Park superintendent
Colonel John White is shown
fourth from left, with the first
unofficial superintendent,
Walter Fry, to his right.

all arable acreage in the foothills, and on February 14th, President Benjamin Harrison signed into existence the Sierra Forest Reserve—more than four million acres that stretched north to Yosemite, east to the Sierra crest, and south to well past Sequoia National Park.

FINANCING THE NEW PARK

It was a national park and forest at its best—a place filled with ice-chiseled canyons and castellated summits; sylvan lakes and riffled rivers; wooded aisles and far-reaching meadows. It was a world where eagles spiraled the heights, jays patrolled latticed shadows, and deer browsed brambly vines. But most of all it was a land that belonged to the people, and by the turn of the century it was becoming increasingly clear that if the people were ever to enjoy that which had been so hard-fought and hardwon, it had to be made accessible.

The problem was money. Up until now, the War Department had borne the expense of operating the two parks, and the budget had not been stretched to include visitor roads or trails. The Kaweah road remained the only readily accessible way into the park, and even it had fallen into disrepair. But hope was on the horizon. In 1901, Congressman James Needham managed to obtain a congressional authorization of $10,000 to be used for improving and protecting Sequoia and General Grant National Parks. By 1903, the Kaweah wagon road had not only been repaired by the U.S. Cavalry under the leadership of Captain Young, but was finished all the way into Giant Forest, and, thanks to the financial support of the Visalia Board of Trade as well as the Mount Whitney Club, trails ribboned the backcountry as far as Kern Canyon and Mount Whitney. It was time to celebrate. And so the people did. In August, more than 300 made the four-day round trip from Visalia to attend the dedication ceremonies.

In 1913, the cavalry gave up its post as "park protector," leaving Sequoia in the charge of its first civilian superintendent, Walter Fry. The task ahead was monumental. To all intents, this was a park that had been little changed in its more than 20 years in existence. Despite the fact that Giant Forest sported a tourist camp and a handful of trails that hairpinned into the backcountry, the park itself remained largely undeveloped, little visited, and pocked by dozens of privately-owned tracts that had been legally acquired under the Swamp & Overflow Act.

STEPHEN MATHER
AND THE NATIONAL PARK SERVICE

The private lands were the greatest concern. Despite requests to Congress by Governor Waterman in 1890, and 22 years of accumulated recommendations by every acting superintendent in army employ, Congress refused to allocate the funds necessary to secure the lands for the park. It seemed certain that sooner or later the owners would subdivide their tracts for summer homes or, worse yet, sell out completely to lumber companies.

Then along came a man who made a difference. His name was Stephen T. Mather, and in the summer of 1914 he was a part of a Sierra Club outing visiting both Yosemite and Sequoia National Parks. Irritated by the poor conditions he found, Mather wrote a protesting letter to a college fraternity brother, Franklin Lane—who just happened

to be the Secretary of the Interior. Lane's reply was short and to the point:

"Dear Steve,

If you don't like the way the national parks are being run, come on down to Washington and run them yourself."

It was a challenge not to be ignored. By 1915, Mather was not only Lane's assistant, but in charge of running the national parks— and one of his top priorities was to effect some changes in Sequoia and General Grant.

Working on the premise that people care more about what they have known or seen, Mather organized and personally paid for an expedition into Sequoia, and among his many influential guests were Congressman Frederick Gillett, ranking Republican on the House Appropriations Committee, and Gilbert Grosvenor, president of the National Geographic Society. It was a trip that would net long-term results. The following year, Mather managed to obtain an option to purchase one of the largest privately-owned tracts inside park borders for $70,000. But where on earth to get the money? As luck would have it, the summer sojourn of 1915

■
The U.S. cavalry shown in front of the General Sherman Tree in 1914, the last year of their tenure in the park.

GEN. SHERMAN

■
*Mather and his assistant,
Horace Albright, encouraged
visitation to the parks to
enlighten the public about
conservation. The auto guide
(above right) was produced
in the first year of the Mather/
Albright administration. Above
Left: Moro Rock was as popular with visitors in the early
part of the century as it is now.
The wooden stairs were replaced by carved steps in the
early thirties.*

DEPARTMENT OF THE INTERIOR
FRANKLIN K. LANE, SECRETARY
NATIONAL PARK SERVICE
STEPHEN T. MATHER, DIRECTOR

SEQUOIA AND GENERAL GRANT NATIONAL PARKS

1917

USEFUL HINTS TO MOTORISTS

These parks are national playgrounds. Observance of the following rules and suggestions will make your visit pleasant and add to the pleasure of others.

The use of automobiles and motorcycles will be permitted on all roads in Sequoia National Park at all hours. In General Grant National Park, however, machines will be permitted only on the Millwood Road, the North Road, and the Stephens Grade Road, and between the hours of 6 a. m. and 7 p. m.

The fee for an automobile or motorcycle permit in the Sequoia National Park is $2.50, and in the General Grant National Park it is 50 cents. These fees are payable in cash only. Permits are good for the entire season, expiring on December 31 of the year of issue.

Careful driving is required at all times.

The speed limit is 8 miles per hour, except on straight stretches of road, where a speed of 15 miles is allowed.

Horns should be sounded when approaching curves, vehicles, pedestrians, or saddle animals.

Muffler cutouts must be closed when passing horses or camps.

Do not drive in the ruts of the road. Observance of this suggestion will do much towards keeping the roads smooth and in good condition, and may save you a broken spring.

Teams have right-of-way at all times, and in all places. If horses appear nervous, automobiles will take the outer edge of the road and engine will be stopped until horses have passed.

Be careful of your camp fires. Thoroughly extinguish them before leaving, by water or covering with earth.

Camp and park your cars only in designated localities—see regulations.

For the protection of yourself and other visitors, your car must be equipped with good brakes, horn, and lights.

THESE ARE NOT THE REGULATIONS. There may be obtained from the rangers at the entrances or from the Supervisor, copies of the regulations for the government of the parks and motor vehicle traffic therein. These regulations are also published in the general circular of information which the park officers have available for free distribution.

SEQUOIA AND GENERAL GRANT NATIONAL PARKS BELONG TO YOU. HELP US TAKE CARE OF THEM.

NOTE.—FOR ADDITIONAL COPIES OF THIS MAP OR FURTHER INFORMATION CONCERNING SEQUOIA AND GENERAL GRANT OR OTHER NATIONAL PARKS ADDRESS THE NATIONAL PARK SERVICE, WASHINGTON, D. C.

---

was about to pay off. In an unprecedented action, Congress authorized $50,000 to purchase private property in Giant Forest—with the decisive vote cast by none other than Congressman Gillett. With money still needed, Mather contacted the National Geographic Society to see if they might be interested in helping preserve the Big Trees. They were. Almost by return mail came a note from Gilbert Grosvenor—and a check for the entire $20,000.

EXPANSION OF THE PARK

Within the next five years, most of the private acreage inside Sequoia's borders was purchased and given over to the park, and when the totals were finally run up, the ledger showed that the National Geographic Society alone had increased park holdings by nearly 2,000 acres at a cost exceeding $96,000. With the issue of private lands finally resolved, Mather focused on expanding Sequoia into the adjacent Kern and Kings Canyon watersheds. However, land here was nearly impossible to appropriate for park purposes. The Forest Service administered it under a multiple use policy and almost everyone inside and outside the valley was standing in line to get at it.

The cattlemen wanted it for grazing; prospectors wanted it for mining; power companies wanted it for dam building; the agriculturalists wanted it for reservoirs; sportsmen wanted it for hunting; and lumber companies wanted its timber. So outspoken and well-organized was the opposition that park expansion seemed nearly impossible. It was then that Mather, now director of the newly established National Park Service, decided to lead a 1916 expedition into the southern Sierra—and this time he routed many influential guests through the heart of the Kings-Kern country.

On March 3, 1917, California Congressman William Kent went before the House with a bill to enlarge Sequoia National Park; in May, California Senator James D. Phelan introduced a matching bill in the Senate. All to no avail. Subsequent bills—of which there were many—were either ignored or defeated, and it was beginning to look like adding the Kings-Kern watersheds to the park was a hopeless situation. Then came the compromise of 1926, a bill that expanded

Sequoia National Park by adding both Kern Canyon and Mount Whitney, but which left the much-contested Kings Canyon area outside park boundaries. With the opposition satisfied by the re-drawn boundaries, and Mather determined to accept any expansion as better than none, the bill rode easily through Congress. On July 3rd, President Calvin Coolidge gave it his official signature —and Sequoia was well on its way to becoming a first-class park.

VISITATION AND GROWTH OF SERVICES

The following year, more than 10,000 visitors made their way into the park's towered wilderness, and with visitation increasing annually, services took an up-swing. By the early 1930s, the wooden steps up Moro Rock had been replaced by a stairway carved into the rock itself and the tent cabins of Camp Sierra in Giant Forest had been torn down and a regular camping area established at Lodgepole. Between 1933 and 1942, the Civilian Conservation Corps built

trails, campgrounds, and service buildings, and the park concessioner modernized and expanded its visitor facilities in Giant Forest.

With Kings Canyon established as a national Park in 1940, and the two parks administered as one by 1942, the California Twins became—in the minds of most—a single unit that seemed almost without end. With so much more to see and do, visitation rose steadily, and by 1954 exceeded a million annually. By the mid-1970s, it was apparent that congestion in the parks' already established sections needed to be alleviated by expanding visitor services into outlying areas. By the end of the decade, the park concessioner, now Guest Services Incorporated, had built a double-storied lodge at Cedar Grove, and between 1983 and 1984 had added an extensive market-gift facility at Lodgepole and a deluxe two-story motel in Giant Forest. The California Twins had, indeed, become first-class parks. And everyone entering their portals knew it.

■
One of the first auto stages to visit the Sherman Tree in 1915.

Top and Bottom: An unknown photographer took these photographs of Indians in Sequoia National Park.

Indian Life

The Spaniards called them Diggers—an ignoble name for the strong and proud Native Americans who inhabited California before the white man came. Their state history goes back more than 12,000 years; their permanent occupancy about 9,000 years; and their time within what is now Sequoia and Kings Canyon National Parks, at least 1,000 years. Whatever their history, one fact remains clear: they were an inventive and adaptable people who fashioned bows and arrows so accurate they were first-shot deadly, wove baskets so tightly they would retain water, and felled trees using nothing more than fire and sharp sticks.

Historically, the tribes of Sequoia and Kings Canyon were peaceable and friendly, and even though their territories were distinctly separate, each tribe had at least some contact with the others. Claiming the entire Kings and Kaweah watersheds were the Western Mono or Monache. To the south, along the Kern River drainage were their shirttail relations, the Tubatulabal; east of the Sierra crest lived their close kin, the Owens Valley Paiute; west, in the San Joaquin Valley, were the Yokuts—completely unrelated yet welcome visitors who came to hunt, trade, or simply gain relief from the valley's unrelenting summer sun.

Largest of the southern Sierran tribes

was the Monache. At 2,000 strong, they spread out from the lowest foothills through the most remote canyons and into the highest passes. Yet their permanent villages were always set at the lower elevations where they could be used spring, summer, and fall. Most extensive of all was Hospital Rock—a thriving village that fared well for untold centuries. But then the white man came. And the death bell began tolling. The many settlers swarming throughout the region brought with them more than pick-axes and shovels. They carried also the dreaded diseases smallpox and measles, and by the time the epidemic of 1862 was over, most of the Sierran Indians were dead. By 1865, the few that had survived had disappeared—absorbed, it was supposed, by the Owens Valley Paiutes.

Though their years here were long, the signs of their passing are few. Most visible are the many granitic rocks and basins potholed by acorn-grinding mortars and the indecipherable pictographs of Potwisha and Hospital Rock. Rainstorms sometimes unearth an obsidion arrowhead or two and now and again a potsherd comes to light. For the most part, however, it remains for the archeologist to tell us where the Indians set their permanent villages and summer camps. Even then, so intertwined are their historic and prehistoric use that even the trained eye often has trouble discerning exactly where it was that yesterday died and tomorrow began. It has been said that the Indians' spirits still roam the land. Maybe it is true. For when the evening mists gather in the canyons and the sky turns to a pink-tinged twilight and all that remains readily visible against the skyline is the stark knob of Moro Rock, there comes on the breeze the sound of whispering voices and soft footfalls and the sharp staccato of rock striking rock. Some will say that it is nothing more than the river rushing, twigs falling, and stones dislodged from some lofty place. But the one suspended in the moment senses more. For over there, in the deepest shadows. . . .

■
Left: Native Americans left a number of pictographs on the granite of the Sierra Nevada. These paintings are carefully conserved today and their whereabouts kept secret. Above: Indians of this area of California used rocks as mortars for grinding their staple food of acorns.

Chapter Four

Flora and Fauna of Sequoia and Kings Canyon

The hordes keep coming. Today, nearly 2 million people a year pass through the two parks and with few exceptions, all head straight for those green empires called Giant Forest and Grant Grove. Not surprising. This is the world of the Big Trees, those ropy-barked showoffs that hypnotize their audience into believing that they are the only things in their realm worth seeing. But not so. Beyond their overstuffed magnificence lies an incredible variety of plants and animals, for these parklands encompass two other life zones—distinct units worlds apart from the 4,500- to 7,500-foot elevations that the giant trees call home.

Only the hardiest hikers or trail riders ever view Sequoia and Kings Canyon's rooftop world, for the land between 8,000 and 14,000 feet is—and shall always be—a trackless wilderness. Much more accessible, but almost always bypassed, is the parks' basement, the foothill region between 1,500 and 4,500 feet in elevation. In this place spring arrives early, summer's heat seems to last forever, winters are short and mild, horizons are often hazy, and six-month droughts are a yearly occurence.

Strange, then, that with all the park to choose from, these oak- and chaparral-covered hills are home to such a wide variety of things that skulk, skitter, creep, crawl, and fly. Most visible is the California ground squirrel, a bushy-tailed lowlander that often shares its burrow with all manner of audacious toads, snakes, or skunks who simply move in and claim squatter's rights. Interestingly enough, the squirrel seems not to care and quietly goes about the business of day to day living—munching manzanita berries or acorns or tender grasses and, on occasion, the entire contents of a quail's nest, including any young that have recently hatched.

Without a doubt, the dubious honor of being the noisiest foothill resident goes to the scrub jay. This blue-gray bird is brash, bright-eyed, and ever on the alert. It spends the entire day flitting hither and yon, screeching at anything that moves or catches its eye. The only time it succumbs to silence is in the vicinity of its own nest, and even that quietude

Opposite: Scenicio flowers in the Sierra Nevada. Above: Brodiaea flowers. Below: A golden-mantled ground squirrel.

is short-lived, for the young are as sassy as the parents and before long the entire family is out policing its scrubby terrain with a flashy determination that is both admirable and comedic.

Most of the creatures that call these undulating hills home are nocturnal and for that reason are seldom seen. White-footed mice while away daylight hours in intricate underground tunnels; bobcats rest in shallow caves; ringtails curl up under rocky ledges or in hollow trees. But when the sun has fallen behind the horizon and the last splash of vermilion is gone from the sky, everything changes. Perhaps it is the cricket chorus that starts things moving, for almost as though their monotonous melody were some sort of alarm clock, animals rouse themselves from the day's rest and begin venturing forth.

It will be a busy night. Coyotes skitter through the oak woodlands looking for ground squirrels; ringtails take to the trees hoping to find sleeping birds; skunks search out likely spots where mice might hide; bobcats cross and recross their territory looking for chipmunks; the gray fox ambushes woodrats and pocket gophers. By the time the thin morning light breaks up the darkness, the foothills are once again serenely quiet—and the only clue that this is a land where life literally clambers over life is the signature footprints left along streamside flats.

■
Above: Yucca and manzanita trees in the dry foothill zone of the park. Right: Indian paintbrush.

THE HIGH COUNTRY

While the foothill climate is truly Mediterranean, the high country weather seems borne out of Alaska. This is a winter-dominated land, and so harsh is the environment that everything that inhabits these rocky reaches has been branded by the elements themselves: sedges and grasses are dwarfed; herbs are plant-pillows barely two inches high; shrubs sprawl along the ground. Yet nowhere is the brand more pronounced than in the foxtail and white-bark pines. For in this place they are both stunted and wonderfully ugly—coniferous gnomes that live on the edge of subsistence and, most of the time, on the brink of perpetual cold.

Farther downslope their counterparts produce handsome, symmetrical forms. But in the land above 10,000 feet they are consistently twisted, with tops dead and spiky, and roots that ramble across stony soil. They are living reminders of their environmental past; and their corkscrew-like shapes tell of the forces that influenced their growth patterns and molded the character of their communities. Every bend, wrinkle, and spirals denotes scream-ing winds and continual desiccation; tem-peratures too cold for extended periods; soil that refused to hold fast; and mois-ture—its abundance or its lack. Yet the feisty trees persist, surviving not so much in spite of adversity but because of it: they slow down their lives, stretching out the process of living, and in the end, encom-pass patriarchal years that belie their size and form.

For the most part, the birds and mam-mals that inhabit these storm-battered heights prefer to live downslope, in and around the treeline. Most often seen is the yellow-bellied marmot, a pudgy little fellow whose piercing whistle not only alerts others of its kind to potential danger, but the rest of the community as well. Its home is usually deep inside a jumbled rock pile, and because it hibernates six months out of every year, it spends most of the summer soaking up the sun and eating till its stomach bulges. By late August it is nearly too fat to move, and around early October it waddles into its den, curls up in a grass-lined nest, puts its front feet over its eyes, and goes into a deep sleep that lasts until March or April.

Not all of the high country critters spend the winter snoozing. Porcupines poke about; so do weasels, pikas, white-tailed jackrab-bits, mountain chickadees, and Clark's nut-crackers. But for the most part, it remains for spring to bring about any great activity, and by summer this world of shortgrassed meadows, sofa-cushion plants, and rock-bound lakes is in full swing. It is now that the intrepid backpackers return, climbing for days to view this sky parlor extraordi-naire. Few who have seen it have ever been disappointed. It matters not that the air here is so dry and thin it seems almost transparent. The result is a sky that borders on purple. And no one cares that the sun shines with an uncommon brilliance. Its unsullied light illuminates a landscape of ice-quarried pinnacles, glacial cirques, and snowmelt streams.

■
Above: The stark landscape of the high country is in sharp contrast to the lower eleva-tions. This contorted foxtail pine clings to the rocky Sierra granite. Left: The peripatetic coyote patrols the park.

The noisy Steller's jay is a ubiquitous presence in the park.

THE MID-ZONE FOREST KINGDOM

Intriguing as the high country and foothill regions are, it is still the mid-zone forests that draw the crowds. Even without the giant sequoias, the parks' mixed conifer forest would be heralded as a champion, for encompassed within this great green wall are at least 10 different evergreen species with names like incense cedar, western juniper, red and white fir, and jeffrey, lodgepole, sugar, and ponderosa pines.

They are a royal court second to none. Nowhere else but in California do so many species grow together, and only in the southern Sierra do they consistently attain such great size. Yet next to the giant sequoia they appear as midgets—hard to believe when you consider that the white fir stretches 200 feet skyward and boasts basal diameters in excess of five feet; and the sugar pine, largest of all the world's pines, stands 180 feet tall, claims diameters of more than seven feet, and produces pendulum-like cones that can weigh as much as four pounds.

Though the mid-zone forest claims many residents, there is one saucy bundle of energy who thinks he owns it all—and constantly proclaims so in a loud, scolding voice. Noisier than most squirrels, the chickaree or Douglas squirrel, spends every waking hour bouncing about the forest, spiraling the trees, and giving anyone or anything who dares to trespass into his supposed territory a piece of his mind. Home is usually an abandoned woodpecker nest; hibernation is out of the question; and the preferred diet is pinecone seeds.

It is the little critter's compulsion for pinecones that has partially contributed to the giant sequoias' reproduction. Because Sierran winters are long, the chickaree depends heavily on pinecone seeds for food, so in late summer or early fall, the furry locomotive climbs to the top of a fir or pine or sequoia and begins chomping down the cones. His speed is remarkable—a single chickaree was once observed cutting 538 cones in 31 minutes—and anyone unfortunate enough to be standing beneath the conifer when the cones begin raining down is usually sorry, especially if the tree is a sugar pine.

Although the chickaree eats the seeds of all other conifers, he consumes only the fleshy scales of the sequoia cones, leaving the seeds themselves scattered along the ground or on top of the snow. Most of the time the seeds just lie there and eventually rot away, for the duff is either too dense or the soil too acidic. But sometimes, when conditions are just right, the seed germinates, and though it appears to be nothing more than a small green freckle atop spring-warmed soil, it has within it the inherent ability to become a patriarch. And all because a greedy little squirrel with messy manners happened to pass this way.

BEAR FACTS

Most visitors pay no attention to the vociferous chickaree. Or to the chipmunks, golden-mantled squirrels, and Steller's jays

■
Above: the harmonious textures of lodgepole pines. Left: Black bear can be found in the forested mid-zone of the park.

■
Top: A bear print in the park. Above: This mule deer is well camouflaged by granite and snow. Opposite: Crescent Meadow in Giant Forest, a popular hiking spot, erupts into a riot of wildflowers in springtime.

so prominent in the sequoia realm. Mule deer are fascinating; so are gray squirrels. But what the visitors really hope to see is a bear. And because the hulking creatures tend to frequent heavily-used or developed areas many get their wish.

Though many believe bears to be primarily nocturnal, they are, in fact, out and about at any time of the day or night, and even though they are called "black" bears, their coloring ranges from ebony to strawberry blonde. Seldom are two adults seen together except during mating season, and even then the time spent in one another's company is short-lived. Cubs, usually two, are born in January, and by the time spring arrives and it is time to leave the den, the naked, blind babies have become furry four-pound balls.

They spend the summer gorging themselves. Insect larvae are tasty; so are carpenter ants, grasshoppers, crickets, gophers, ground squirrels, and all manner of wild berries. By the time autumn rolls around, mom and her fat little rough-and-tumble offspring head for their winter den. They will stay together nearly two years—for that is how long it takes the female to teach her cubs how to paw-fish the creeks, rip open rotting logs to find grubs, dig out underground rodents, and climb trees to escape danger.

Because the animals and plants here are both complicated and intriguing, Sequoia's first civilian superintendent, Walter Fry, instituted a naturalist program with the hope that if visitors better understood what they were seeing, their time spent in the park would be more meaningful. It was a program that worked. Today a host of fulltime and seasonal naturalists share the wonders of Sequoia and Kings Canyon with all who attend their nature walks or campfire talks. The participants learn about sequoia ecology and Sierra geology; how to read animal tracks and where to take the best photographs; why meadows exist and how to read a topographic map.

The programs are both fun and informative. But more than that, they instill in the participant a sense of belonging to the land and once that happens, the visitor is no longer just a traveling sightseer, but an avid park protector. Walter Fry would have been pleased.

Chapter Five

Assessing the Future

Almost from the very beginning the national parks were, by congressional decree, areas set aside to "conserve the scenery and the natural and historic objects and the wildlife therein and to provide for the enjoyment of the same in such manner and by such means as will leave them unimpaired for the enjoyment of future generations." In administering that policy, park officials did everything in their power to protect the land entrusted to them from change, and just to be on the safe side, a policy of total fire suppression was instituted throughout the system. It was not a tactic that worked well at Sequoia and Kings Canyon.

By the 1960s, it was obvious that sequoia reproduction was nearly at a standstill. Not surprising. The sequoias could hold on to their cones for as long as 20 years awaiting the time when fire would race through the grove, dry out the cones, and allow the seeds to filter onto the fresh mineral soil where they would germinate. With fire no longer a part of the scene, sequoia seedlings became few and far between, and even those that did somehow manage to germinate seldom made it through the initial stages.

Something had to be done. In 1968, Sequoia and Kings Canyon instituted a fire management plan that was unprecedented in the National Park Service. No longer was theirs a policy of total suppression, but one of controlled prescribed burns. The wisdom of the plan has become obvious, and nowhere more so that in the sequoia groves themselves. Here, carefully monitored fire has eliminated tons of forest litter—explosive caches that, should wildfires have struck, would have turned the groves into blazing infernos. But even more than allowing easy access by eliminating litter, the fires have caused the cones to release their horded seeds onto fresh mineral soil, and within the last 20 years, the regeneration in the park's less-trampled groves has been remarkable.

There is yet another man-caused problem facing the park, and its nature is such that a solution must be found. Smog formulated in the San Joaquin Valley does not stay there. Air currents carry it into the Sierra uplands, and the result is not only distorted vistas and

■

Top: A researcher evaluating ponderosa pine for ozone injury symptoms. Above: Acid rain sampling station at Emerald Lake (9,000' elevation). Bottom: An endangered peregrine falcon. Opposite: Lupine and sequoias in Muir Grove.

unhealthy air, but a definite impact on park resources. To better understand exactly how the pollutants are affecting Sequoia and King Canyon—and the Big Trees in particular—the Park Service has established a comprehensive monitoring program in which pollution levels and patterns are documented as well as ozone levels recorded and their effects determined. In time, the facts of pollution and park resources will be clear, and when that happens the findings will be turned over to the state and federal agencies involved in auditing air quality.

Unfortunately, not all of the park's man-related problems have solutions. The grizzly, which once hulked along the Sierra mid-elevations was hunted and annihilated, and by 1922, even those within Sequoia and General Grant's protected borders had disappeared. Other park inhabitants fared little better. The vast herds of bighorn sheep that ranged along the Sierra crest and throughout the Great Western Divide in the 1800s were quickly decimated by hunting, disease, and domestic competition into two remnant herds that are few in number and seldom seen; and though southern bald eagles and peregrine falcons sometimes soar high above the parklands' granitic battlements, their presence is but a transient treat.

MAN AND NATURE

These problems underscore the truth of the saying, "No man is an island unto himself." What man does in one place today affects men in all places tomorrow, and as a nation we are finally beginning to achieve the cultural maturity that recognizes that fact. In the meantime, we can look over our shoulder and see clearly that we have either misused or destroyed much of what was once our natural heritage, and were it not for men like George Stewart, John Muir, and Stephen Mather, who mobilized thousands of our forebears to action, we would, today, have few—if any—places left in which to seek asylum from an overcrowded and overstressed world.

Yet because of these early conservationists, bits of yesteryear remain. Our western parks are echoes in time, and though they may not be wholly as they once were, they are still places where glaciers cling to shady cirques and snowmelt thunders down a thousand creeks; where steep granite walls squeeze rivers into froth and white-plumed waterfalls punctuate cliff faces; where tundra plants bloom with arrogant assurance and columned trees soar into the temple blue. Such a place is Sequoia and Kings Canyon. Some say it is a picture of America as it once was; others claim it is America at its best. This is, perhaps, the one time when everyone is right.

Visiting Sequoia and Kings Canyon Today

Stay awhile. Walk the spongy paths beneath the fluted trees, climb to the top of Moro Rock and revel in the view, drive to the bottom of Kings Canyon and investigate 200 million years of Earth-history etched in stone, backpack into the high country's beautifully disordered tableau. Explore a cave, fish a stream, wade a creek, capture wildlife on film. Absorb the magic—and when you leave, a bit of it will go with you.

VISITOR SERVICES AND PROGRAMS

A full range of visitor services and accommodations are operated throughout Sequoia and King's Canyon by Guest Services. The largest selection of motels, cabins, bus tours, horse corrals, food services, and gift shops are located in Giant Forest and Grant Grove. Markets, laundry facilities, gifts, and gasoline are also available at Lodgepole and Cedar Grove. For more information on park facilities write: Guest Services, P.O. Box 789, Three Rivers, CA 93271 or call (209) 561-3314.

The parks' 14 campgrounds are all first-come, first-served with the exception of Lodgepole, which is on the Ticketron reservation system. All have water, tables, and toilets. Those campgrounds at Lodgepole, Grant Grove, and Cedar Grove have public showers as well. For information on campgrounds or backcountry permits write: Sequoia and Kings Canyon National Parks, Three Rivers, CA 93271 or call (209) 565-3341.

The Park Service maintains visitor centers at Ash Mountain, Lodgepole, and Grant Grove—as well as an information booth in Giant Forest. Ranger stations are located in Mineral King and Cedar Grove. The ranger stations deal mainly with questions on backcountry travel and wilderness permits and, like the visitor centers, cater to those who want to know where to go and what to see in a couple of hours or less. The visitor centers also offer movies and

■
Above, Top to Bottom: This sign was carved by the Civilian Conservation Corps in the thirties; The Studio in Giant Forest Village sells Indian arts and crafts; one of the rustic rooms in The Lodge in Giant Forest Village. Right: Crystal Cave, on the way to Giant Forest, is a wonderland of stalactites and stalagmites.

slide shows as well as extensive exhibits on geology, Indians, early settlers, mining, sequoia ecology, park preservation efforts, and the years of army administration. During summer months, ranger-naturalists conduct daily walks, talks, and evening programs on the parks' flora, fauna, geology, and ecology; during spring and fall, the programs are on weekends only. Locations and topics are listed in the parks' free newspaper, *The Sequoia Bark,* available at all entrance booths, visitor centers, and ranger stations.

TRAVEL TRIVIA
AND MOUNTAIN MANNERS

There are no freeways in Sequoia and Kings Canyon. Because the topography here is up and down, in and out, and round and about, so, too, are the roads that dissect its wilds. The General's Highway, which begins in Ash Mountain and ends 50 miles later at Grant Grove, is the best of the lot—and even it is narrow, steep, switchbacked, and in many places, devoid of guardrails. The road up the South Fork Canyon of the Kings River into Cedar Grove is little better: the paved two-lane drops off steeply on one side, is edged by

sheer granite walls on the other, and has
few pulloffs. Spur roads into the wonderfully scenic Mineral King and the much-
admired Crystal Cave of stalactites and
stalagmites are asphalted one-lanes that
must accommodate two-way traffic; both
are extremely steep, hairpinned, and—in
some places—in ill repair. All park roads
deserve careful navigation, and though it
sometimes seem easier to round out the
corners by cutting them just a bit, it is
important to remember that doing so may
result in a head-on collision.

There is more to insuring a wonderful
visit than just careful attention to switchbacked roads. Learn to recognize poison
oak and stay away from it, lest you end up
feeling like a million mosquitoes bit you all
at once. Drink only water that comes from
a tap, for the parks' many waterways are
home to *Giardia lamblia,* an invisible
protozoan which, if ingested, will not be
fatal—though you will certainly feel like
it is going to be. Campground beggars such
as chipmunks and ground squirrels are
so appealing it is tempting to offer them
human treats. Remember though, that all
park animals are wild and sometimes bite
the hand that feeds them. Also, rodents are
hosts to fleas that sometimes carry plague.
Learn how to prevent—and cure—hypo-
thermia, a serious condition caused by
the body core cooling down too fast; and
remember that the top of Moro Rock is
not a great place to be if a thunderstorm
threatens, for objects projecting high above
the surrounding landscape often become
natural lightning rods.

The national parks and other areas of primitive wilderness with their virgin forests and their original plant life and wildlife have been bequeathed to us by the generation we have succeeded. We, too, must fulfill our trust during our time, and deliver these superb areas unimpaired to the generation following ours.

Robert Sterling Yard